Weird Pets

By Heidi Adelman

The Child's World
www.childsworld.com

Published in the United States of America by The Child's World®
1980 Lookout Drive • Mankato, MN 56003-1705
800-599-READ • www.childsworld.com

ACKNOWLEDGMENTS

The Child's World® : Mary Berendes, Publishing Director

Produced by Shoreline Publishing Group LLC
President / Editorial Director: James Buckley, Jr.
Designer: Tom Carling, carlingdesign.com
Cover Design: Slimfilms

Photo Credits
Cover–iStock (3)
Interior–Corbis: 8; dreamstime.com: 13, 15, 18, 21, 23, 26, 29; iStock:
5, 7, 11, 14, 17, 20, 24; Photos.com: 16, 25; Tammy Rao: 10, 19.

LIBRARY OF CONGRESS CATALOG-IN-PUBLICATION DATA

Adelman, Heidi.
  Weird pets / by Heidi Adelman.
     p. cm. — (Reading rocks!)
  Includes index.
  ISBN-13: 978-1-59296-862-6 (library bound : alk. paper)
  ISBN-10: 1-59296-862-7 (library bound : alk. paper)
 1. Pets—Juvenile literature. I. Title. II. Series.

SF416.2A34 2007
636.088'7—dc22

                              2007004206

CONTENTS

THOSE CUTE Critters

Millions of people have pets. These animal friends share good times and bad—and eat the occasional shoe. Most of those pets are dogs, cats, or maybe fish. But if those pets are not your thing, then you've come to the right place! There's a weird world of pets out there for you to choose from. Let's start by meeting some unusual **mammals**.

Ferrets are long and skinny and furry—kind of like a big fuzzy scarf. Using their sharp teeth, wild ferrets hunt and kill smaller animals for their food. Pet ferrets need a diet with lots of meat in it as well. You can buy ferret food in the pet supply store.

Ferrets are happy, active pets who need lots of attention. They need a large cage with toys and a bed and places to hang out.

Ferrets like to play with other ferrets, so you might want to think about getting more than one. This way they can keep each other company.

Ferrets need time out of their cage to play with you every day, too. Since they're hunters, they have sharp teeth, so you'll have to play with your ferret carefully.

How about a chinchilla? If you have one, you can watch it take a dust bath. Every day, your chinchilla will climb into a pile of dust and roll around in it, flapping and shaking. The dust helps remove oil that builds up on their skin.

What makes an animal a rodent? Rodents are mammals that have sharp front teeth, usually on top, that are used for grinding or gnawing.

These active little pets like to climb and hide and explore the areas outside their cage, too. They'll need plenty of play time.

Chinchillas are **rodents**, which

means they need to chew on things. They need a big, sturdy cage with toys that they can't nibble into little pieces. They'll need hard branches to chew on to keep their teeth healthy.

Feed your fuzzy little chinchilla hay, special chow, fruits, and vegetables.

If you only think pigs are big, pink animals that like to live in mud, think again. Pot-bellied pigs are dark-skinned and sort of hairy. They're also smart, easy to train, curious, playful, and clean. They're very quiet pets, and many people love them. You can teach these pigs

This picture shows a good example of why these pigs got their name!

Performing Pigs

Pigs are among the smartest animals around. They can be trained to walk on leashes, slam dunk basketballs, play piano, play soccer, jump through hoops, dance, ride skateboards, and do lots of other tricks.

to do tricks. They love their families and hate to be alone. So why doesn't everyone have a pot-bellied pig for a pet?

First, they grow to be about 125 pounds (57 kg). So these weird pets need a lot of space! Plus, they eat like, well . . . pigs. They can learn to open the refrigerator and cabinets and knock over trash cans. They beg for food, and scream when they want more. Pot-bellied pigs need very patient owners!

You may think all furry pets are cuddly, but hedgehogs are not. Yes, they do have soft fur on their bellies. But they also have short, prickly **spines** on their backs. When they feel scared, hedgehogs roll up into a tight little ball with the spines poking out. This way, bigger animals can't eat them.

Pet hedgehogs need a big cage

They won't play fetch, but your hedgehog will sit gently in your hand.

with places to exercise, a litter box, a nice bed, and places to hide. They eat insects, and think that mealworms are the best treat ever. There are also special hedgehog foods you can get at a pet store.

Hedgehogs can grow to be 5 to 8 inches (13 to 20 cm) long.

Most hedgehogs don't like to be held, but they don't mind being picked up sometimes. Sometimes they climb all over their owners!

COLD-BLOODED Critters

What if mammals aren't for you? How about a **reptile** or an **amphibian**? Here are some different pets that might be right for you.

Some of the most popular reptile pets are leopard geckos, because they're friendly little lizards. A leopard gecko is yellow and white with black spots.

A 20-gallon (76-l) glass tank is the right size for two or three leopard geckos. But make sure there is only one male in the tank. Males will fight each

other. Your geckos will need some things to climb on and some boxes or a cave to hide in. Geckos also need a warm spot to lie in during the day.

Feed your geckos crickets and worms. You'll notice that your geckos have fat tails. This is where they store fat for when they don't have enough food to eat.

Leopard geckos can grow to about 8 to 10 inches long (20 to 25 cm). Some types can live to be 20 years old!

One guess where fire-bellied toads got their name!

Pet frogs can live 4 to 15 years, and some have been known to live even longer.

Frogs are not cuddly pets. In fact, it's not a good idea to hold them very much. For the most part, frogs just sit around waiting for food to wander by. But they make those froggy sounds, and they are ugly in a cool way. Plus, you get to feed them live insects!

The tricky thing about keeping frogs as pets is making their home comfortable for them. Some frogs spend their time in water, some on land, and some both places. If you get a frog, you'll need to know how it lives. Then you can set up a tank that seems just like its own **habitat**.

Good choices for your first pet frogs include dwarf frogs, Oriental fire-bellied toads, White's tree frogs, African clawed frogs, American green tree frogs, and Pacman frogs (yes, they're named for the video game!).

This green tree frog is sitting on a flower. You can see its smooth, shiny skin.

Salamanders live secret lives. They spend a lot of their time hiding in dark places. And their skin is very sensitive—just holding them can sometimes hurt them. However, with a little work, you can make a nice home for a salamander.

Spotted salamanders like this one live on land.

Like frogs, different salamanders live in different kinds of habitats. The best salamander pets are the ones that live on land.

Land salamanders like their home to be damp, so you'll need a tank with leaves or moss on the bottom. The tank should also have a little pool, perhaps made by filling a shallow dish with clean water. Salamanders like to have areas where it's light and areas where it's dark (such as little caves). They may dig tunnels in their tanks, too.

Adult salamanders eat insects such as crickets and worms.

Salamanders come in many colors, such as this red salamander. Most can grow to be between 7 and 14 inches (18-35 cm) long.

If you're thinking about a pet snake, a corn snake is a good choice. They're gentle and easy to take care of, and they don't get so big that they'll scare your grandma. Plus, they come in bright colors and many beautiful patterns.

Corn snakes make safe and interesting pets.

Corn snakes grow to be about four feet (122 cm) long and live 20 years or more. They can live in a glass tank with a secure top. Snakes are great escape artists, so make sure to keep the lid on tight! They'll need something soft in the bottom of the tank and some places to hide. They'll also need a warm spot and a cool spot so they'll always feel just right.

Corn snakes like to eat mice and small rats. An adult corn snake is easy to feed—it eats just once a week! Corn snakes like to eat both fresh and frozen mice. You can get both at the pet store.

This corn snake's home is made to look a bit like its habitat in the southeastern United States.

Bearded dragons spread out the spines on their face to appear bigger and fiercer.

Bearded dragons are reptiles that come from Australia. They have little spines all along the bottom of their neck that they stick out if the lizards feel afraid. The idea is that this "beard" will make them look too big and too scary to eat.

Light Like the Sun

Bearded dragons need special lights that give them all the different kinds of light. This is just like the light they would get from the sun. Without this special light, they will die. Pet supply stores sell these reptile lights.

Bearded dragons grow to be almost
two feet (61 cm) long and can live
up to 10 years. They eat bugs and
vegetables, and are very friendly—
for lizards, that is. Some might take
the bugs right out of your fingers.

Baby bearded dragons are only about the size of a person's finger.

Bearded dragons can live happily
in a very large glass tank. They'll
need stuff to climb on and some
warm places and some cool places
in the tank. This helps them keep
their body temperature just
right. You can also spray
them lightly with
water to help.

OTHER WEIRD
Pets

The mammals didn't interest you? Snakes and frogs and lizards creep you out? Don't worry, we've got even more weird pets to look at.

Hermit crabs sometimes live near beaches. You might see them skittering around on the sand. Believe it or not, they might be looking for something that people also look for on beaches— seashells. Hermit crabs don't grow their own shells, so they have to find a shell to live in. Part of the fun of keeping hermit crabs is giving them interesting shells. As your hermit crab outgrows of one shell, you can get it a bigger one to live in.

Hermit crab tanks should have sand on the bottom, something to climb on, and some damp and dry spots. Hermit crabs eat special crab food, plus fruits and vegetables.

A hermit is a person who likes to live alone, and hermit crabs are not hermits at all. They are very friendly and social, and like to live with other hermit crabs.

Put different kinds of shells in your hermit-crab tank. Then you can watch them move from "house" to "house."

23

What about a pet spider? Don't be scared! Tarantulas are quiet and clean. They don't need a big cage, and they don't make any noise. Of course, they're giant, hairy spiders, but maybe you don't mind that. There's one other thing—tarantulas bite when they're scared. It's best not to pick up or hold a pet tarantula. The spider is happiest (and safest) when it's in its tank.

Female tarantulas can live to be more than 20 years old, but the males live just a few years. A small glass tank makes a good tarantula home. They like it warm and dark, with a special hiding place.

Tarantulas are hunters, and they eat cockroaches and other insects. You can also feed them small mice or put fish in their water bowl.

Nasty but Not Deadly

Although a tarantula bite has **venom**, it's not very strong. So it will hurt and swell up, but it won't kill you. Also, some tarantulas have special hairs on their belly that have little **barbs** on them. When you touch the hairs, they stick into your skin and make it very itchy.

Every part of a stick insect's body helps it hide from predators.

Don't forget pet insects! There are several insects that make interesting pets. One of the most unusual is the stick insect. They look like sticks so **predators** won't see them hiding among real sticks. The sticks they hide in help provide food, too. Stick insects like tasty leaves. They also like to eat different grasses.

A predator is an animal that eats other animals.

Stick insects can live in a glass tank, as long as they are warm and the tank has a lid.

They live a long time for insects, too—about a year.

Stick insects are not cuddly, but you can hold them in your hand. Carefully pick them up by the body (not the legs!) and let them stand on your palm.

Stick Figure

According to the *Guinness Book of Records*, a stick insect holds the record for world's longest insect. One was measured at more than 12 inches (4 cm) at a zoo in England.

If you startle an ordinary cockroach, it will run away. But if you startle a Madagascar hissing cockroach, it will make a loud hissing sound. The males also hiss at the females as a way of inviting them to mate. They hiss at each other when they are getting ready to fight, too. And sometimes, a whole group of Madagascar hissing cockroaches will all hiss at the same time. Nobody knows why—maybe they just have a lot to say.

You can keep five or more cockroaches together in a small glass tank with a lid. They'll need something to dig into on the bottom, something to climb up on, and a little sponge or cotton ball to get

Madagascar hissing cockroaches live about three years.

water from. They like to eat dog food and rotten fruit. Yum!

The next time you and your family are thinking about getting a new pet, don't just go for a boring old cat or dog. Think weird!

Hissing cockroaches not only look weird, they sound weird, too!

GLOSSARY

amphibian a cold-blooded animal that can live both on land and in the water

barbs sharp points that stick out from something

habitat the place where a wild animal lives

hermit a person who likes to live alone, away from all other people

mammals animals that have warm blood, bodies with hair, and that feed their babies milk

predators animals that eat other animals

reptile an animal that has cold blood and scaly skin

rodents animals with special front teeth that never stop growing

spines sharp, stiff objects on the bodies of certain animals

venom poison-like liquid that is present in spider bites

FIND OUT MORE

BOOKS

The ASPCA Complete Guide to Pet Care
by David L. Carroll (Plume, New York) 2001
A big book of animal care that covers dogs, cats, birds, fish, reptiles, and amphibians.

Exotic Pets: From Alligators to Zebra Fish
by John Zeaman (Franklin Watts, London) 1999
Facts and stories about weird animals that some people keep as pets.

Great Pets! An Extraordinary Guide to Usual and Unusual Family Pets
by Sara Stein (Storey Publishing, North Adams, Mass.) 2003
A fun book that covers all kids of pets.

An Instant Guide to Small Pets
by Cecilia Fitzsimons (Gramercy, New York) 2000
A helpful guide to caring for pet snakes, frogs, and even spiders.

WEB SITES

Visit our Web page for lots of links about weird pets:
www.childsworld.com/links

Note to Parents, Teachers, and Librarians: We routinely check our Web links to make sure they're safe, active sites—so encourage your readers to check them out!

INDEX

Heidi Adelman grew up with a variety of pets, both weird and ordinary. She has been writing about animals and editing books about them for 20 years. She currently has three cats, all of whom are weird in their own way.